Go for it!

Workbook

SECOND EDITION

Ken Beatty
with Martin Milner

HEINLE
CENGAGE Learning™

Australia • Brazil • Japan • Korea • Mexico • Singapore • Spain • United Kingdom • United States

Go for it!:Workbook 3, Second Edition
Beatty, Milner

Editorial Manager: Berta de Llano

Development Editors: Margarita Matte

Director of Marketing, ESL/ELT:
  Amy Mabley

International Marketing Manager:
  Eric Bredenberg

Production Manager: Sally Giangrande

Sr. Print Buyer: Mary Beth Hennebury

Project Manager: Kris Swanson

Interior Design: Miguel Angel Contreras
  Pérez; Israel Muñoz Olmos

Illustrators: Iñaki (Ignacio Ochoa Bilbao),
  Jaime Rivera Contreras

Composition: Pre-Press Company, Inc.

Photo Manager: Sheri Blaney

Photo Researcher: Melissa Goodum

Cover Designer: Linda Beaupre

ISBN-13: 978-1-4130-0026-9

ISBN-10: 1-4130-0026-6

Heinle
20 Channel Center Street
Boston, MA 02210
USA

Cengage Learning is a leading provider of customized learning solutions with office locations around the globe, including Singapore, the United Kingdom, Australia, Mexico, Brazil, and Japan. Locate your local office at **www.cengage.com/global**

Cengage Learning products are represented in Canada by Nelson Education, Ltd.

Visit Heinle online at **elt.heinle.com**

Visit our corporate website at **www.cengage.com**

Photo Credits: Unit One, Page 5: ©Ron Chapple/Taxi/Getty; Unit Three, Page 13: ©Docwhite/Taxi/Getty; Unit Four, Page 17: Top left, ©Chris Cole/Photographer's Choice/Getty; Unit Five, Page 22: ©Janis Christie/Photodisc Green/Getty; Unit Eight, Page 34: ©Cheque/CORBIS; Unit Thirteen, Page 60: Top left, ©TO'Keefe/PhotoLink/Getty; Top left center, ©Greg Epperson/Index Stock Imagery, Inc.,; Top center, ©PhotoLink/Getty; Top right center, ©Karl Weatherly/Getty,; Center right, ©AEF/Mark Buccaill/The Image Bank/Getty; Unit Fourteen, Page 65:© Trevor Wood/Stone/Getty; Unit Fifteen, Page 67: Top left: ©Michael Edwards/Stone/Getty; Top left center, © Matthias Clamer/Stone/Getty; Top right center, ©Yellow Dog Productions/Photographer's Choice/Getty; Top right, Yellow Dog Productions/The Image Bank/Getty; 2nd row top left, ©Photodisc Collection/Getty; 2nd row top left center, ©Stockbyte Gold/Getty; 2nd row top right center, ©Ryan McVay/Photodisc Green/Getty; 2nd row top right,©Comstock Images/Getty; Unit Sixteen, Page 72: ©Orion Press/Stone/Getty

Printed in the United States of America
8 9 10 11 12 13 21 20 19 18

Table of Contents

Unit 1 LESSON A
I'm not as shy as Pedro.

1 Write the words in the correct column. Then add some other adjectives to the chart.

noisy
crazy
shy
friendly
outgoing
energetic
funny
serious
calm

Adjectives with *-er*	Adjectives with *more*
longer healthier	more expensive

2 Complete the sentences. Circle *True* or *False*. Then check your answers in *Go for it!* Student Book 3, page 1.

1. Tom is (tall) __taller__ than Tina.   (True)   False
2. Jack is (energetic) _____ than Grace.   True   False
3. Pedro is (quiet) _____ than Tom.   True   False
4. Tina is (outgoing) _____ than Pedro.   True   False
5. Jack is (crazy) _____ than Tom.   True   False
6. Jack is (serious) _____ than Tina.   True   False

Terry

Trudy

Lilly

3 Write sentences comparing the three teens.

1. __Terry is more serious than Trudy.__
2. _____
3. _____
4. _____

4 Look at the chart and make sentences using *not as . . . as.*

	quiet	friendly	dependable	athletic
Jim	☆☆	☆☆	☆☆☆	☆☆☆
Jane	☆	☆☆☆	☆☆	☆
Gina	☆	☆	☆	☆

1. __Jane is not as quiet as Jim.__
2. _____
3. _____
4. _____

5 Write the questions for the answers below.

1. Question: __Are you as studious as Sally?__

   Answer: No, I'm not as studious as Sally. She's more studious than me.

2. Question: _____

   Answer: Yes, I'm as tall as Andrew. In fact I'm taller.

3. Question: _____

   Answer: No, Paula is really clever.

4. Question: _____

   Answer: Yes, my new boyfriend is much cuter than my last one.

6 Use the chart to answer the questions.

	band	description	talented
Fred	The Dunkers	drummer	☆☆
Paul	The Poms	lead singer	☆☆
Slam	The Dunkers	lead singer	☆☆☆
Liz	The Poms	drummer	☆

1. Who's Fred? Is he as talented as Liz?
   __He's the one who's the drummer for the Dunkers. He's more talented than Liz.__

2. Who's Paul? Is he more talented than Slam?

   _____

3. Who's Slam? Is he as talented as Paul?

   _____

4. Who's Liz? Is she as talented as Fred?

   _____

LESSON B He has a great personality.

7 Unscramble the sentences.

1. quieter / sister / than / my / am / I   <u>I am quieter than my sister.</u>
2. both / they're / outgoing _____
3. than / athletic / you're / more / Jim _____
4. dependable / more / brother / my / I'm / than _____
5. is / crazy / not / he _____
6. than / my / I / am / sister / friendlier _____

8 Read the article about two brothers, Ali and Ahmed. Then answer the questions.

The Soccer Twins

Are all twins exactly the same? No, they're not! Ali and Ahmed are twin brothers. They look the same and in some ways they are the same. But in other ways they are very different. Ali and Ahmed are both very athletic. Ali and Ahmed both like soccer. But Ali is a bit wild and plays soccer every day. Ahmed only plays on weekends. Ali and Ahmed both have friends, but Ali is more outgoing than Ahmed. Ahmed is also more studious and reliable. However, they are both fashionable and popular.

1. Which one is Ali?
   <u>Ali is the one who is a bit wild and outgoing.</u>

2. Which one is Ahmed?
   _____

3. In what ways are they the same?
   _____

4. In what ways are they different?
   _____

Twin qualities?
Some identical twins like to dress and appear exactly the same way. Some do not and go out of their way to appear as different as possible. But twins who have been separated at birth and raised in separate families often make the same choices and act in similar ways.

9 Write a paragraph about two friends or family members. Compare the two people using words from this unit.

_____
_____
_____
_____
_____
_____

Go for it!
Families

Read the article and underline the adjectives.

Birth Order Theory

A lot of people believe that your place in the family says a lot about your personality and your chances for success in life. This birth order theory suggests that the first child is likely to be more serious and hardworking than children born later. The reason is that first children tend to work harder to please their parents. Another belief is that the youngest child is likely to be more outgoing and funny. The middle child, on the other hand, is likely to be unhappy as he or she is overlooked between other siblings.

Some studies done more recently, however, suggest these beliefs aren't true. Scientists have found that other things are more important. For example, children from small families do best in school. This might be because they get more help at home. Also, only children seem to be the most studious.

Use the information in the article to match the phrases.

1. The youngest child
2. The middle child
3. The oldest child
4. An only child
5. A child from a small family

a. does slightly better in school.
b. is more hardworking.
c. is often unhappy.
d. is often funny.
e. is the most studious.

Write the names of three children in your family or another family. Write descriptions and decide if they fit the birth order theory.

	name	description	fits/doesn't fit
oldest	_____	_____	_____
middle	_____	_____	_____
youngest	_____	_____	_____

Unit 2 LESSON A
First switch on this light.

1 Check the columns to match the words with the actions.

	a key	a light	a dollar bill	a button	a door	a machine
switch on		✓				✓
push						
turn						
plug in						
insert						

2 Match the solutions with the problems.

Problem

1. It's very dark.
2. The computer won't switch on.
3. I can't print this document.
4. It's hot in here.
5. How do I open the door?

Solution

a. Slide it. Don't push it!
b. Press the print button.
c. Switch on the light.
d. Plug in the electric cord.
e. Open the window.

3 Use the words in the box to fill in the blanks. Then put the instructions in the correct order.

> Press
> Type
> forget
> Insert
> Take

☐	_____	your money.
☐	_____	the button that says **Withdraw $20.**
☐	_____	your Personal Identification Number.
1	_Insert_____	your card.
☐	Don't _____	your card!

4 Write the words under the correct picture.

coin
money
juice
soda
dollar
coffee
ticket
water
cup of water
can of soda

Count words	Non-count words
coin	money

5 Use the clues to complete the crossword puzzle.

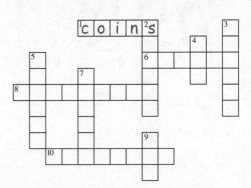

Across

1. some pieces of money
6. _____ your card into the machine.
8. My card has a _____ strip.
10. It is a _____ telephone card.

Down

2. The light is turned off. Please _____ it on.
3. Press the red _____.
4. The door is locked. Where is the _____?
5. I only have bills. Do you have some_____ for the machine?
7. After you're finished, don't forget to _____ your card.
9. Your paper is still under the photocopier _____.

6 Read the instructions. Then read the sentences and circle *True* or *False*. Rewrite the false sentences to make them true.

This is the new library photocopier. You do not need to use coins or bills. Instead, you use a card with a magnetic strip. Insert the card in the orange slot. Lift the lid and put your paper down. Now press the blue button to make your copies. After you have finished, don't forget to remove your card.

1. You can use coins but not bills.   True   False
   _____
2. The new photocopier is for the school.   True   False
   _____
3. The card has a magnetic strip.   True   False
   _____
4. Press the orange button to make the copies.   True   False
   _____
5. You lift the lid before putting your paper down.   True   False

LESSON B **Now add the flour.**

7 Circle the word that does not belong in each group.

1. oil	flour	milk	water
2. pizza	tacos	butter	sandwich
3. flour	salt	sugar	bowl
4. cheese	pancakes	butter	milk
5. knead	cover	mix	pepperoni

8 Look at the pictures and write a sentence to describe each step shown of how to make a loaf of bread.

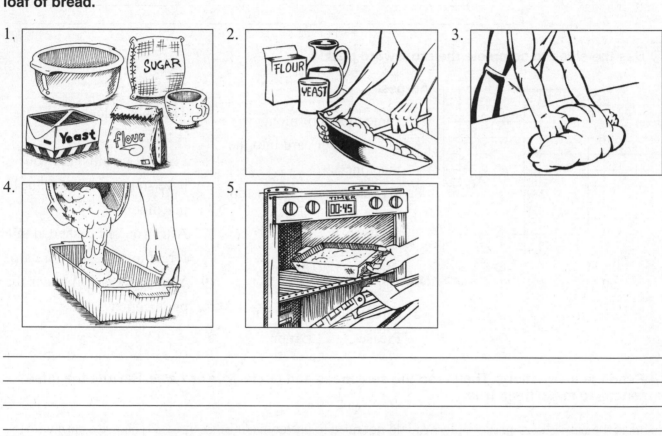

_____
_____
_____
_____
_____

9 Write about how to do another simple task, like making tea, coffee, or your favorite food. Make sure you include at least five steps.

_____
_____
_____
_____
_____

Go for it!
International measurements

Read about the Metric and American Standard systems. Then convert the amounts.

In most of the world, the metric system is the popular way to measure quantities as well as area and speed. Metric measurements in cooking include grams, milligrams, liters, and milliliters. American Standard measurements include teaspoons, tablespoons, cups, quarts, and pounds.

American Standard	Metric
1 teaspoon	5 milliliters
1 tablespoon	15 milliliters
1 cup	236 milliliters

1. 3 teaspoons = _____
2. 4 cups = _____
3. 2 tablespoons = _____
4. 1/2 cup = _____
5. 7 teaspoons = _____

Read the list of ingredients for pancakes. Write the amounts using Metric Standard.

1 egg
1 cup milk
1 tablespoon vegetable oil
1 1/4 cups flour
2 teaspoons baking powder
2 tablespoons sugar
1/2 teaspoon salt

1. _____
2. _____
3. _____
4. _____
5. _____
6. _____

Try making pancakes at home!
Break the egg into a bowl. Stir in the milk and vegetable oil. Add the flour, sugar, baking powder and salt. Mix these ingredients. Put a little cooking oil in a frying pan and heat the pan. Pour some pancake batter into the pan. When bubbles form on top of the pancake, turn it over. Cook the pancake until it is golden brown on both sides.

Unit 3   LESSON A
I went on a fund-raising walk.

1 Write the words in the correct column.

tough
special
tedious
tiring
awesome
rewarding
inspiring
fantastic
depressing
fascinating

Positive	Negative
special	tough

2 Read the story and then rewrite it in the past.

Every Christmas, we go to the Springfield School for Special Children. We make toys and small presents and then take them to the kids. There are 32 children in the school and every child gets a present. We also play with and talk to the kids although some of them don't understand everything. It is a lot of work but it is very rewarding.

Last Christmas, Class 8 went to. . . .

3 Write the questions for the answers below.

1. Q: Did you go to school today?
   A: No, I didn't go to school today.

2. Q: _____
   A: It was a fantastic day.

3. Q: _____
   A: We walked from the school to the hospital.

4. Q: _____
   A: Yes, my team thought it was interesting.

5. Q: _____
   A: No, she didn't think it was very challenging.

6. Q: _____
   A: I helped my friend's charity.

4 Match the phrases to make sentences.

1. My school wants to raise money   a. service.
2. It's part of our community   b. challenging.
3. We walked around   c. for charity.
4. It was extremely   d. to the hospital.
5. We gave the money   e. the lake.

5 Look at the picture and read the false sentences. Write true sentences.

Last Saturday

1. False: Last Saturday, the teenagers didn't do any community service.

    True: _____

2. False: No one read storybooks.

    True: _____

3. False: Two girls sold hamburgers.

    True: _____

4. False: One teenager painted a picture.

    True: _____

5. False: The children thought the teenagers were depressing.

    True: _____

6 Read the letter. Then answer the questions.

1. Why was Andrew surprised?

    _____

2. Where do the kids go to school?

    _____

3. What did Andrew do to help?

    _____

4. Where did Andrew volunteer?

    _____

5. Why was Andrew volunteering?

    _____

```
Dear Rachel,
Today I went to the Hospital for Disabled
Children to volunteer as part of my
Community Service Day. I thought it would
be quite depressing, but I was wrong.
Actually, many of the kids are quite
inspiring. They have big problems and
tedious lives, but they make the most of
it. They do many unusual and fun things.
They have to do all their schoolwork at the
hospital so I helped one girl read her
English book. My day was awesome. You
should try it sometime.
Andrew
```

LESSON B **I had a great day!**

7 Look at the picture and write four sentences about what each of the kids did.

One girl played the piano to the old people.

_____

_____

_____

_____

8 Use these words to write sentences in the past tense.

1. speak / woodworking / class / yesterday _____

2. camping / take / seven / kids _____

3. sell / tacos / make / money / volunteer / group _____

4. have / toys / children / hospital _____

5. yesterday / friends / make / meals / sick / people _____

6. Thursday / go / school / story-telling time _____

9 Write a paragraph about community service done by someone you know. Use some words from the box.

What did you do to help?

| went |
| sold |
| took |
| made |
| saw |
| spoke |
| had |
| got |

Go for it!
Save the dolphins

Read the article and summarize the problem in one sentence.

Save the Dolphins

Dolphins are friendly animals. They enjoy being with other animals in the ocean. Sometimes they swim up to people who are swimming in the ocean, and they often follow boats. Dolphins also swim along with large schools (groups) of tuna, and this causes a problem for the dolphins. Fishing companies use helicopters and speedboats to locate dolphins because the dolphins often follow large schools of tuna. Then fishing boats use extremely long nets to catch the tuna and take them to factories that make canned tuna. Often dolphins are caught in the nets along with the tuna. The people on the fishing boats throw the dolphins back in the ocean, but many dolphins die anyway. The problem is that dolphins are not fish. They are mammals, like dogs, cats and people. Mammals breathe air. When the nets cover the fish and dolphins underwater, the dolphins can't get air. They often die before the net is pulled up.

In the 1980s, tuna fishing boats killed 100,000 dolphins a year. Most U.S. tuna fishing boats now use fishing methods that don't kill dolphins. Do you want to help save the dolphins, too? Look for a "dolphin-safe" label on the tuna you buy at the store.

Use information from the article to answer *True* or *False*.

1. Dolphins are dangerous animals.   True   False
2. A "school" is a name for a group of fish.   True   False
3. Dolphins are fish.   True   False
4. Dolphins breathe air.   True   False
5. Tuna often swim with groups of dolphins.   True   False
6. Fishing companies use helicopters to locate dolphins.   True   False
7. In the 1980s, tuna fishing killed 10,000 dolphins a year.   True   False
8. Most U.S. companies stopped killing dolphins.   True   False

Write *mammal* or *fish* after each word.

1. tuna _____
2. dog _____
3. shark _____
4. goldfish _____
5. dolphin _____
6. cat _____

Unit 4

LESSON A
I want a job that lets me travel.

1 **Match the words to make an occupation.**

1. airline   a. programmer
2. baseball   b. host
3. computer   c. player
4. talk-show   d. engineer
5. software   e. pilot
6. travel   f. agent

2 **Cross out the word that does not belong.**

1. Q: Maria, what kind of job ~~does~~ do you want when you grow up?

   A: I want a job work that is not a nine-to-five job.

2. Q: Does that mean means you want to work nights?

   A: Yes. I'm not going to be a disc jockey.

3. Q: A disc jockey! That is sounds awesome.

   A: Yes. But it doesn't pay a lots of money.

4. Q: But is it its creative?

   A: Yes, the it is.

5. Q: What kind of job do you want wants?

   A: I want a the job that pays a lot of money.

3 **Look at the pictures. Use the phrases in the box to write about the teens. Then draw and write about yourself.**

| lets you work with numbers   is creative   is not a nine-to-five job   lets you travel |
| pays a lot of money |

Andrew   Susan   Tristan   Terry   Me

Andrew wants to be a soccer player. He wants a job that pays a lot of money and lets him travel.

_____

_____

4 Use the clues to complete the crossword puzzle.

```
[h][e][a][l][t][h]
```

Across

1. Doctors work in _____ care.
3. Travel agents work in _____.
5. I can't play. I need to _____.
6. Teachers work in _____.
7. Computer programmers work in _____.

8. Most people want a healthier _____.
9. The football player works in _____.

Down

2. The dancer works in _____.
4. The talk-show host works in _____.

5 Read the article. Then answer the questions.

Teens talk about their future.

We talked to four teens about what they are going to do in the future. Some of their ideas may surprise you. We asked each person, "What are you going to do when you grow up?" Here are their responses:

Linda
I'm going to study a lot of math and science. I enjoy both of these subjects. When I finish college I'm going to be a computer programmer.

Jim
I'm going to be a professional basketball player. I know that it will be difficult but there is nothing else I want to do. I really love basketball and I know I can be great.

Carol
I'm going to be a singer and dancer. I already take dance lessons after school on Wednesdays. And next year, I'm going to take singing lessons. You're going to see me on TV someday.

Toshio
You know what I'm going to be when I grow up? I'm going to be a father. I'm going to take my kids camping and help them with their schoolwork. What could be more important than that?

1. What kind of lessons is Carol going to take? _____

2. What is Toshio going to do with his children? _____

3. What does Linda want to be? _____

4. What is Jim going to be? _____

LESSON B **I'm going to study harder.**

6 Match the problems with the resolutions. Then write sentences.

Problem

1. I'm too fat.
2. Ivan plays too many computer games.
3. Mary is getting bad grades.
4. My sister and brother are always fighting.
5. I am disorganized.

Resolution

a. study harder / watch so much TV
b. keep a weekly planner / leave my homework until the last minute
c. read more / buy any more games
d. try to get along better / annoy each other
e. lead a healthier lifestyle / eat junk food

1. <u>I'm too fat. I'm going to lead a healthier lifestyle and I'm not going to eat junk food.</u>
2. _____
   _____
3. _____
   _____
4. _____
   _____
5. _____
   _____

7 First read the paragraph. Then go back and fill in the missing words.

going   airline   forget   math   travel   organized   classes   buy

This is your captain speaking

When I grow up, I want a job that let's me (1) _____ and see the world. So I'm going to be an (2) _____ pilot. To be an airline pilot you have to be very (3) _____ and you have to get good grades in (4) _____ and science. Unfortunately, I'm not very organized and I'm not very good at math. So, this is what I'm (5) _____ to do. I'm going to take extra math (6) _____ in the afternoon. That way my grades will improve, I hope! Also I'm going to (7) _____ a personal organizer and write down all the things I usually (8) _____. See you in the skies!

8 Now write a similar paragraph about yourself.

_____
_____
_____

Go for it!
Running
the distance

Many people try to improve themselves in different ways. Lots of people like to lead a healthier lifestyle and exercise more. Read about two people who push themselves physically. Then answer the questions.

Most of us can run half a mile. Some of us can run a whole mile or even two or three miles. But how many people can run 50 miles? Or 100 miles? People who run races of 50 miles or more are called "ultra long distance runners." Ultra long distance races can take as long as ten days to complete.

In 1988, a 50-mile race was held in London, England. The winner was Don Ritchie, who completed the course in just under 4 hours and 52 minutes. Eleven years earlier, in 1977, Ritchie had completed a 100-mile race in just over 11 1/2 hours. Don Ritchie became one of the fastest men alive.

Another amazing runner is Yiannis Kouros. He was the world's fastest runner of races that are more than 100 miles long. Kouros sometimes runs as much as 1,000 miles! Here are some of his best racing times: 200 miles–27 hours and 48 minutes; 500 miles–105 hours and 42 minutes; 1,000 miles–250 hours and 30 minutes. That's over 10 days of running.

1. _____ ran a 100-mile race in less than 12 hours.

2. _____ ran 500 miles in a little more than 100 hours.

3. The 1,000-mile race took over _____ days to complete.

4. It took Yiannis Kouros a little less than _____ hours to run 200 miles.

5. It took Don Ritchie a little less than _____ hours to run 50 miles.

Look at the distances and write what places are that far away from you.

1. _____ is one mile from my _____.

2. _____ is two miles from my _____.

3. _____ is five miles from my _____.

4. _____ is ten miles from my _____.

5. _____ is twenty miles from my _____.

Review 1

1 Write sentences comparing Jim, Liz, and Deng.

	Jim	Liz	Deng
energetic	***		**
quiet		***	*
friendly	**	*	***
dependable	*	***	**
athletic	*		***
crazy	***		*

1. Deng is more energetic than Liz, but she is not as energetic as Jim.
2. _____
3. _____
4. _____
5. _____
6. _____

2 Jim, Liz, and Deng are planning a party for some young children. Number the sentences to make a conversation.

_____ **Deng:** Food, games, and songs. Sounds great. What food are we going to make?

_____ **Liz:** Well, first we are going to need food. Lots of food. And then we can play some games and maybe sing songs.

_____ **Liz:** What about candy apples? Kids love candy apples.

_____ **Jim:** Candy apples sound good. I can sing and play the guitar. What do you think?

_____ **Jim:** OK, everybody. What are we going to need for the party?

_____ **Deng:** Sure. I know lots of kids' games. Sounds great! Let's go for it!

_____ **Liz:** OK. But don't play too loud! Deng, do you know any kids' games?

3 Read the conversation. Then complete the crossword puzzle.

Liz: Okay, let's make the candy apples.

Deng: Sure, how (3 across) apples do we need?

Liz: Let me see. There are (2 down) to be 10 kids so we are going to need 13 apples.

Deng: (4 down) thirteen?

Liz: One for each kid and one for us!

Deng: Of course. Now (4 across) do we do?

Liz: First, put the sugar and the water in a pan.

Deng: Okay, how (3 down) sugar and water?

Liz: 10 tablespoons of (1 across) and the same of water. Mix them together and then heat them for about 10 minutes in the pan.

Deng: Easy! Then we put the sticks in the apples, dip the apples in the sugar and leave them to cool.

Liz: That's it! Thirteen (5 across) apples ready to go. You got the idea.

4 After the party, Liz had a chat with her friend Natalia on the Internet. Read the conversation and change the verbs to the past tense.

Natalia: How's it going? Where (1) (go) _____ today?

Liz: We (2) (have) _____ a great day. I (3) (go) _____ with Deng and Jim to a kids' party.

Natalia: A kids' party! Why (4) (go) _____ to a kids' party? Sounds boring!

Liz: No, we (5) (organize) _____ the party. We (6) (make) _____ candy apples at home and then (7) (take) _____ them to the party. The kids (8) (love) _____ them.

Natalia: What (9) (do) _____ at the party. Games and stuff?

Liz: Yes. Deng (10) (play) _____ games with the kids and Jim (11) (take) _____ his guitar and sang some songs.

Natalia: Hey! Why (12) (not invite) _____ me? It sounds cool.

Liz: Okay. Next time.

5 Write the question or the answers.

1. Q: Who is more active, Jim or Liz?

   A: _____

2. Q: _____

   A: Deng is going to be a physiotherapist.

3. Q: _____

   A: They made candy apples for the party.

4. Q: _____

   A: Ten kids went to the party.

5. Q: What did Jim do at the party?

   A: _____

6. Q: Which is your favorite teen, Jim, Liz, or Deng? Why?

   A: _____

Unit 5

LESSON A
Could you please clean your room?

1 Check the columns to match the words with the actions.

	your bed	the dishes	the floor	your clothes	the living room	the wastepaper basket
clean		✔			✔	
make						
iron						
vacuum						
empty						
put away						

2 Complete the sentences. Use the phrases in the box.

1. A: ___Could you please___ make your bed?

   B: ___Sorry, I can't.___ I'm too tired.

2. A: _____ use the car?

   B: _____ Your father needs it.

3. A: _____ clean your bedroom?

   B: _____ I'm too busy.

4. A: _____ empty the wastepaper basket?

   B: _____ I have to study for a test.

5. A: _____ go to the movies?

   B: _____ And I'll go with you.

> Yes, sure.
> Sorry, I can't.
> Yes, you can.
> No, you can't.
> Could you please
> Could I please

3 Answer the questions. Use the words in parentheses.

1. Q: Could you please clean your room? (Sorry / do the dishes)

   A: ___Sorry, I can't. I have to do the dishes.___

2. Q: Could I please borrow the car? (No / do laundry)

   A: _____

3. Q: Could you please make your bed? (Yes / sure)

   A: _____

4. Q: Could I please use the car? (No / need it this morning)

   A: _____

5. Q: Could you please empty the wastepaper basket? (sorry / iron clothes)

   A: _____

4 Look at the picture and write a list of chores to be done.

_____

_____

_____

_____

5 Use the words in the box to complete the paragraph.

chores	rug	dust	basket
bookshelf	vacuum	wastepaper	laundry

My mom always makes me do so many ___chores___. First, she told me to put my books back on my _____. The _____ was so clean under the books that she told me to _____ the rest of the rug. After I put the books on the bookshelf, she said I needed to _____ it! I dusted it and picked up the old papers and put them in the _____ basket. Then she told me to take out the wastepaper _____. Behind the wastepaper basket were some dirty clothes. So now I'm doing the _____.

6 Write sentences using the pictures.

1. ___I couldn't check the tires._____

2. _____

3. _____

4. _____

5. _____

6. _____

LESSON B Could I invite my friends over?

7 Number the sentences to make a conversation.

___ First, did you put clean sheets on your bed? Second, did you put the dirty sheets in the laundry?

___ Gas? Oh, can I have some money then?

_1_ Hi, mom. Can I have the car keys?

___ I want you to clean the windshield, check the tires, and fill the car up with gas.

___ I'm not sure. Did you do your chores?

___ Mm. OK. But I want you to take the car to the gas station.

___ No, not yet. Can I do it later?

___ The gas station? Why?

___ What chores?

___ Yes, I do. Is that OK?

___ You want to borrow the car?

8 Read the article. Then answer the questions in complete sentences.

Family Chores

This is part three in our series of stories about family life. We interviewed two students, Josh Franklin and Alice Gomez, about their weekend chores. They told us about the chores they did last weekend.

On Saturday morning, Josh had two big chores to do. He didn't like washing the clothes but he enjoyed cleaning out the garage. "I listened to the radio and sang my favorite songs while I worked," he said.

Alice had to go to the store and buy food on Saturday morning for a party on Saturday afternoon. Her mother usually goes with her but this time she went alone. "I liked shopping for food. I bought drinks and snacks. I bought a gift for my sister, too. But I needed a CD player. Josh said I could borrow his CD player. He said he could bring some music, too."

Josh and Alice both liked helping with their parents' yard sale. "I liked talking to all the people," said Josh. Alice said, "My parents gave me part of the money. Now I can buy anything I want."

1. Did Josh have chores to do? _____

2. What did he do while he worked? _____

3. What did Alice buy? _____

4. Did Alice go with her mom? _____

5. What did Josh and Alice both like? _____

The job market

Look at the chart. It shows ten of the fastest growing jobs. Which job is growing the fastest? Which job is growing the slowest?

Job growth 1996–2006

Occupation	1996 employment	2006 employment	Number of added jobs	Percentage of added jobs
cashiers	3,146,000	3,677,000	530,000	17
computer programmers	506,000	1,025,000	520,000	103
general managers	3,201,000	3,677,000	467,000	15
registered nurses	1,971,000	2,382,000	411,000	21
salespersons	4,072,000	4,481,000	408,000	10
truck drivers	2,719,000	3,123,000	404,000	15
home health aides	495,000	873,000	378,000	76
teacher aides	981,000	1,352,000	370,000	38
nursing aides	1,312,000	1,654,000	333,000	25
receptionists	1,074,000	1,392,000	318,000	30

Answer the questions.

1. Which job will have 25 percent more workers in 2006? _____

2. Which job area will gain the most employees? _____

3. Which three jobs are related to health? _____

4. Which areas will have over 300,000 new jobs in 2006? _____

5. How many teacher aides will there be in 2006? _____

Write these numbers in words.

1. 506,000 _____

2. 333,000 _____

3. 1,645,000 _____

4. 2,719,000 _____

5. 15% _____

Unit 6

What's the best movie theater?

1 Check the columns to match the words.

	seats	movies	screen	snacks	tickets
the widest variety of		✔		✔	
the most comfortable					
the cheapest					
the biggest					
the best					

2 Look at the words in parentheses. Make comparisons by using *most* + the word, or by adding *-est* to the word

1. (comfortable) This club is the _____ in town.

2. (big) This is the _____ supermarket.

3. (loud) This CD shop has the _____ music.

4. (cheap) This concession stand has the _____ food.

5. (wide) This movie theater has the _____ screen.

6. (convenient) This movie theater is the _____ to the bus stop.

3 Unscramble the sentences.

1. closest / park / this / is / home / to / the

   <u>This is the park closest to home.</u>

2. of / food / the / restaurant / variety / that / has / most

   _____

3. they / the / chair / bought / comfortable / most

   _____

4. girl / Maria / in / popular / class / most / is / our / the

   _____

5. is / sound / the / loudest / school's / system / our

   _____

6. much / this / is / restaurant / better

   _____

> **Cheap?**
> **Cheap** is a less polite way of saying something is **inexpensive** or **doesn't cost too much.**

> **Most or -est?**
> **Most** or **-est** words are called superlatives.
> Short words add **-est**, e.g., cheapest, prettiest
> Longer words use **most**, e.g., most expensive, most comfortable

4 Use the chart to write sentences with superlatives.

	Multiscreen	Alta Vista	Maximedia
ticket prices	$10	$12	$10.50
number of films showing	8	4	10
distance from home	2 blocks	20 minutes walk	15 minutes in the car
comfortable seats	*	***	*
quality of concession stands	**	**	***

1. _Multiscreen has the cheapest seats._
2. _____
3. _____
4. _____
5. _____

5 Use the words in the box to complete the paragraph.

| variety   best   good   comfortable   biggest   better   cheapest   loudest |

Most people think that all movie theaters are the same. Most are (1) _____, but the one I go to is (2) _____. First, it's the (3) _____ place in town and has the (4) _____ sound system. That's important when you go to an action movie. The tickets are cheap. In fact, they are the (5) _____ in town. The concession stand has a great (6) _____ of snacks and the seats are (7) _____. The (8) _____ thing is that I live next door!

6 Look at the pictures and make comparisons using words from this unit.

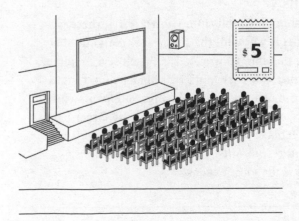

_____

_____

_____

_____

LESSON B Who do you think was the funniest?

7 Write sentences using the opposites.

| dull / creative | quiet / loud | funny / boring | shy / outgoing | energetic / lazy |

1. <u>Trevor is the dullest and Elsa is the most creative.</u>
2. _____
3. _____
4. _____

	Trevor	Toshio	Elsa
dull	***	**	*
quiet	**	***	*
funny	*	**	***
shy	***	**	*
energetic	**	*	***

8 Read the paragraph about shopping malls. Then write a similar paragraph about three other places that you know, for example, CD stores, sports stadiums, clothes / sports shops, schools, etc.

First . . .
When you begin a sentence with **first**, the second clause or sentence should begin with **second**. At the end, you can use **finally**.

Shopping Malls

There are three shopping malls in my town. First, there is the Grand Vista. It is very old, the shops are small and dirty, and it is not very popular. However, it is the closest to home. Second, there is the New City Mall. It is bigger than Grand Vista, it has more shops, and it has the biggest cinema with the widest variety of movies. Finally, there is the Green Valley Complex. This is the newest mall in town, and it has the best shops and restaurants. It is my favorite mall. Unfortunately, it is the most expensive.

Place _____

_____

_____

Go for it!
Movie history

Read the article. Then make notes next to the dates.

Movie History

When Spanish explorers first came to the area now called Hollywood, Native Americans were the only people living there. By the 1870s, there were many farms there that grew bananas and pineapples. The Hollywood area had a warm, sunny climate and, in the 1880s, people from other parts of the United States started to build "winter" houses in Hollywood.

In 1894, Thomas Edison invented the Kinetoscope. This machine let one person at a time look at a moving picture. Soon inventors learned how to project these moving pictures onto a wall so that many people could watch the images at one time. By 1895, people all over the world were watching "movies."

Hollywood's open spaces and sunny weather made it a perfect place for movie makers. In 1911, the Nestor Company opened Hollywood's first film studio. Soon Cecil B. DeMille and D.W. Griffith began making movies in the same area. During the next 20 years, Hollywood became the movie-making center of the world.

- 1870 _____
- 1880 _____
- 1894 _____
- 1895 _____
- 1911 _____

Circle *True* or *False*. Rewrite the false statements.

1. No one lived in Hollywood before the 1870s.   True   False

   _____

2. Hollywood has a warm climate.   True   False

   _____

3. People built summer homes in Hollywood in the 1880s.   True   False

   _____

4. Many people could watch moving pictures together   True   False
   on a Kinetoscope.

   _____

5. The Nestor Company started Hollywood's first film studio. True   False

   _____

6. D.W. Griffith was a Hollywood farmer.   True   False

   _____

There will be less pollution.

1 **Write the number of the corresponding sentence in the correct column.**

1. There will be no wars.

2. We'll travel around the world by space shuttle.

3. There will be no schools.

4. People will live to be 200 years old.

5. There will be no cars.

6. Cancer and AIDS will be eradicated.

7. We'll learn by swallowing knowledge pills.

8. There will be less pollution.

9. There will be more people.

10. The United Nations will become more important.

Education	World events	Transport	Medicine

2 **Number the sentences to make a conversation.**

__ But how will kids use them? The letters will be too small.

__ For one, they will have a lot more computers.

_1_ In the future, what do you think schools will be like?

__ In what ways will they be different?

__ Kids will just talk to their computers. And their computers will talk back!

__ No, each student will have his or her own computer.

__ Oh, the computers will be the size of a telephone.

__ Well, schools will be much different than today.

__ Yes, each classroom will have a few computers.

__ You think so? Where will they keep them?

3 **Match the phrases to make sentences.**

1. When people eat better food and take more exercise,

2. When there are more electric cars,

3. When there are robots in every house,

4. When my children go to school,

5. When people learn to get along better,

6. When there is better public transport,

a. there will be more time for leisure activities.

b. there will be fewer wars.

c. there will be fewer cars.

d. there will be less pollution.

e. they will be healthier.

f. there will be fewer books and more computers.

4 Using information from the chart, fill in the blanks in the sentences below. Use *more, less,* or *fewer.*

Littleton, New York

Now	In 100 years	In 200 years
600 houses	1,000 houses	1,000 houses
a lot of pollution	almost no pollution	no pollution
seven schools	two schools	no schools
2,400 people	3,500 people	2,800 people
a lot of snow	little snow	no water
six movie theaters	two movie theaters	no movie theaters

In 100 years . . .

1. there will be ___more___ houses.
2. there will be _____ pollution.
3. there will be _____ schools.
4. there will be _____ people.
5. there will be _____ snow.
6. there will be _____ movie theaters.

5 Write short answers to these questions. Use information from the chart above.

1. Will there be more snow in 200 years? _____
2. Will there be fewer schools in 100 years or 200 years? _____
3. Will there be fewer people in 200 years? _____
4. Will there be less pollution in 100 years or 200 years? _____
5. Will there be more movie theaters in 200 years? _____
6. Will there be more houses in 200 years? _____

6 Read the paragraph about "The Present" and then write about "The Future."

The Present

At the moment, many people live in cities. There are very few electric cars and so there is a lot of pollution. The air is dirty and many people have lung disease and other health problems. As a result, the government spends a lot of money on health care, and there are a lot of hospitals. People have little time for leisure activities, and their health is bad, which in turn means people need more hospitals, and the government has to spend more money on preventable problems.

The Future

In the future, fewer people will _____
_____
_____
_____
_____

LESSON B When I get my license, I'll be able to drive.

7 Read the article. Then answer the questions.

> Children today will be able to do many more things in the future. They probably will not go to school. They will be able to study at home on computers. They will not take buses to theaters. Instead, they will be able to travel by monorails but not by space shuttles. That will be too expensive. They will be able to learn different languages by taking a few pills. Children of the future won't be able to go to movie theaters. There won't be any!

1. Will children do fewer things in the future?

   _____

2. Where will children go to school in the future?

   _____

3. Will children take buses in the future?

   _____

4. Will children be able to travel by space shuttles in the future?

   _____

5. Will children go to more movie theaters in the future?

   _____

6. Why won't there be any movie theaters?

   _____

8 Look at the picture and write about the things that Melissa will be able to do.

_____ driving a car

_____ playing chess

_____ playing the cello

_____ flying in a space suit

9 What things will you be able to do in the future?

1. In six months, I will be able to _____.
2. In one year, I will be able to _____.
3. In two years, I will be able to _____.
4. In five years, I will be able to _____.
5. In ten years, I will be able to _____.

Go for it!
In space

Read about a space elevator. Then read the sentences and circle *True* or *False*.

What's the tallest elevator ride you've ever been on? Can you imagine an elevator a mile high? A space elevator sounds like wild science fiction but it's a serious project being pursued by NASA and others. It is expected that such a project will be completed by the year 2100. The space elevator would be the biggest machine people have ever made. Its base tower, 30 miles high would sit on the Earth's equator–much higher than anything ever built. The cable for such an elevator might be 90,000 miles long, one third of the distance to the moon. This would allow a space shuttle racing up it to make use of Earth's spin to reach Mars in a matter of weeks, not months.

1. A space elevator has been built on the equator.	True	False
2. The cable for the elevator will be 90,000 kilometers long.	True	False
3. The space elevator will be completed in the next century.	True	False
4. The space elevator would need an enormously tall base.	True	False
5. The space elevator has only been considered by NASA.	True	False
6. The space elevator would allow for quicker trips to Mars.	True	False

Here are four questions that NASA is trying to answer. Rank them in order of importance to you. Then write your reasons.

_____ a. How did we get here?

_____ b. How did stars and galaxies form?

_____ c. Are there other planets like the Earth?

_____ d. Do other planets have conditions suitable for the development of life?

_____

_____

_____

What amazing new things do you think will happen in the next 100 years?

_____

_____

_____

Unit 8

1 Write the careers in the correct column.

physiotherapist   basketball player   accountant   computer programmer   rugby player   writer
graphic designer   disc jockey   chef   politician

Might become famous	Will never become famous

2 Number the sentences to make a conversation.

☐ And here's an outstanding actress.

☐ *1* Is this your autograph book?

☐ Mm. Let's see. Peggy Lee?

☐ No, I don't.

☐ No, it's my friend's autograph book.

☐ No. He won two Academy Awards.

☐ Oh, it's Sally's.

☐ Peggy Lee won three Academy Awards.

☐ She's sensational! You don't know her?

☐ Tom Hanks! Wow. He won an Academy Award.

☐ Twenty-three! That's a lot.

☐ Yes. Here's Tom Hanks.

☐ Yes. Sally has autographs from twenty-three actors and actresses.

3 Complete the conversation. Use the words in parentheses.

1. A: _Excuse me, could I have your autograph?_ (have / autograph)

   B: Yes, you can. Where do you want me to write?

2. A: _____. (here / autograph book)

   B: OK. Here you are. That's my autograph.

3. A: _____ (think / your movies / sensational)

   B: Oh, good! Which movie did you like the best?

4. A: _____ (last movie / *Falling Leaves* / creative)

   B: Sorry. That was another actor's movie.

4 Use information from the box to write sentences.

The Bootleggers

lead singer and guitar	Peter Dought	born 1973–murdered 2001
bass guitar	"Swing" Lowe	born 1972
drums	Justin Thyme	born 1970
formed	1988	
first hit single recorded	1990	
last CD released	1994	
disbanded	1996	

1. _The Bootleggers were formed in 1988._
2. _____
3. _____
4. _____
5. _____
6. _____

5 Use the words in the box to complete the paragraph.

Award
actress
Academy
autograph book
beautiful
born

One year I went to the _Academy_ Awards. I wanted to meet a _____ actress. I took my _____ and looked for an actor or _____ to write in it. Then a little girl stopped to ask me a question, "Where is the Academy Award show?" She was young. Perhaps she was _____ a few years after me. I answered her question. I didn't know her! That night, she won an Academy _____!

6 Write a paragraph about David Beckham. Here are some words and facts to help you.

talented	kind
handsome	expensive
brilliant	bad
intelligent	good

David Beckham	
born	2nd May 1975
signed by Manchester United	1993
selected to play for England	1996
awarded Young Player of the Year	1997
chosen as England captain	2000
bought by Real Madrid	2003

_____
_____
_____
_____

LESSON B When I get my license, I'll be able to drive.

7 Check ✓ the words that definitely go together. Write an ✗ for the ones that definitely don't go together. Write a ? for the ones that are possible but unusual.

	car mechanic	doctor	actress	athlete
creative	?	?	✓	✗
attractive				
kind				
unusual				
famous				
beautiful				

8 Read the article. Then write the questions or answers below.

A Talented Family

Some families are very talented in an outstanding way. The Bremmer family included two parents and seven children. All of the children started learning music when they were two or three years old. They became famous musicians. Marcus and Stephen, born in 1957 and 1959, were famous violinists. Another son, Richard, born in 1955, recorded three CDs of guitar music. Their four sisters were all very beautiful. The oldest and most attractive one was Elsie, born in 1960. She worked as a model and became a famous movie actress. Her three other sisters were also creative. Angela, born in 1962, and Merta, born in 1963, were both writers. The last sister, Tania, born in 1965, was the most creative. She was an artist.

And what about the parents? Both were loving and gentle teachers. The father was a music teacher and the mother was an English and art teacher. It's not surprising that they had such an unforgettable family.

1. Q: Who was the oldest child?

   A: _____

2. Q: _____

   A: Marcus was born in 1957.

3. Q: _____

   A: Tania was the most creative.

4. Q: Who was the most attractive?

   A: _____

5. Q: _____

   A: They were both teachers.

Go for it!
Fame

Read the article and answer the questions.

Fame and the Famous

It has been said that some people are born famous, some people achieve fame, and some people have fame forced on them.

Members of royal families are famous from the day they are born. Even when they are children they are followed by photographers.

Those who become famous include sports players, movie stars, politicians, TV personalities, etc. These people usually enjoy being famous and they like to see themselves in newspapers and on TV.

Then there are the people who have fame forced on them. These people do not want to be famous. They just want to do good and lead a quiet life. But because they are so good they become famous. For example, Mahatma Gandhi was a very quiet man who did not want to be famous. He wanted to help his country and its poor people. He once said, "The best way to find yourself is to lose yourself in the service of others."

Finally, there are the infamous. These are people who have become famous for the bad things they did, for example, the infamous English murderer Jack the Ripper, the American Mafia chief Al Capone, and many others.

1. How many groups of people are mentioned? Name them.

   _____

2. Which group or groups of people probably don't like being famous?

   _____

3. Who else has achieved fame? Think of sports players, movie stars, or others.

   _____

4. Why is Mahatma Gandhi famous?

   _____

5. Would you like to be famous? Why?

   _____

What are the advantages and disadvantages of being famous?

Advantages	Disadvantages
lots of money	can't go out in public unrecognized
_____	_____
_____	_____
_____	_____

Review 2

1 Liz and her mom are having a conversation. Number the sentences to put it in order and write in the names.

_1_ _Liz_: Could Natalia and I go to the cinema this afternoon?

____ ____: Good. But listen. First, could you help me clean the car?

____ ____: OK. I'll wash the dishes first, then I'll pick up my room.

____ ____: I already changed the sheets yesterday.

____ ____: OK. But could you move the car? I can't wash it when it's in the garage.

____ ____: Sure, but first you have to do your chores.

____ ____: Of course I can. Now, where are the keys?

____ ____: And could you put clean sheets on your bed?

2 Read the movie ads. Then write the missing words in the conversation.

The Aliens When the aliens come, what will YOU do? Starring Alan Hudson and Gina Thomas Directed by Gert Huslbecker. Awarded Best Director. **Lost Love** You will cry. You will sigh. Starring Lucy Stevens and Ivor Green. Nominated for 3 Oscars. **Mr. Pea Goes to Town** The Funniest—the Craziest—the Best Comedy Film of the Year. Starring Mr. Pea himself.	was romantic more awarded best three interesting Could

Natalia: Which film shall we see? What about *Mr. Pea Goes to Town*?

Liza: Oh no! That's for kids. (1) _____ we see something (2) _____ serious? *The Aliens* is directed by Gert Huslbecker. He's one of the (3) _____ directors. He was (4) _____ Best Director two years ago.

Natalia: Mmmm. Well, what about *Love Lost*? It (5) _____ nominated for (6) _____ Oscars.

Liza: Ugh. I don't like (7) _____ films. No, *The Aliens* looks the most (8) _____.

Natalia: OK, but let's check the film review first.

3 Read the film review and circle the correct words.

The Aliens

**** Review written by David Goldstein.

We all know that one day we _1. (will / going to)_ make contact with aliens from another part of the universe. But what will happen? Most of us imagine that the Earth will _2. (is / be)_ destroyed, and that we will all _3. (die / live)_ However, director Gert Huslbecker, who was _4. (award /awarded)_ an Oscar two years ago, thinks differently. Maybe the aliens will be friendly, maybe we will be the aggressive ones. Possibly the _5. (most / more)_ exciting science fiction film of the year.

4 Liz and Natalia are buying snacks before the film. Look at the clues in the conversation and use them to complete the crossword puzzle.

Natalia: Could I have some (1 down) please?

Salesperson: Sure. (6 across), medium, or small?

Natalia: Large. And (3 across) I have some butter on it?

Salesperson: Sure. Is that enough?

Natalia: A little (2 across). Thanks.

Liz: And could I have an ice cream, please?

Salesperson: What (5 down)? We have orange, (7 across), apple . . .

Liz: Lemon, please.

Salesperson: With syrup?

Liz: Please! Just a (4 down).

```
                          1.p
                    2.[ ][o][ ][ ]
                          [p]
                    3.[c][ ][ ][ ][ ]
           4.[ ]   5.[ ][o]
                    6.[ ][r][ ][ ]
               [ ]     [n]
           7.[ ][ ][ ][ ]
```

5 Liz writes in her diary every day. She doesn't use full sentences. She writes in note form. Read the diary entry. Then write out the sentences.

Saturday

Morning. Did chores. Picked up bedroom. Washed dishes. Mom couldn't find car keys— couldn't wash car. Able to clean out sand. Try to finish tomorrow.

Afternoon. With Natalia. Went to see *The Aliens*. Really interesting film. Earth invaded by aliens. Surprise! Aliens nicer than humans. Aliens killed by humans. Interesting and a little sad.

Evening. Went to party with Natalia. Very noisy. Went back to Natalia's. Fewer people, less noise. Tomorrow try to clean car.

I did my chores this morning. First I picked up my bedroom. Then _____

_____

_____

_____

_____

_____

_____

_____

_____

_____

_____

6 Write questions or answers.

1. Q: Did Liz dust the bookshelves?
   A: _____

2. Q: _____
   A: No. She couldn't wash the car.

3. Q: _____
   A: They went to see *The Aliens*.

4. Q: What did Liz do on Saturday evening?
   A: _____

5. Q: Which film looked the most interesting to you. Why?
   A: _____

My reading journal 1

1 **Complete the journal page.**

1. Title: __Spider (Part 1)_____

2. Author: _____

3. Setting (where the story happens): _____

4. My favorite character is _____ because _____
   _____

5. The character I don't like is _____ because ____
   _____

6. I think the story is _____ because _____
   _____

2 **Match the columns to make statements that are true about the story. Then write your own true statements.**

1. Pablo,   who is from Romania,   calls his host mother *Mom*.

2. Sophie's mom,   who is from Germany,   lives with Billy, Junko and Stomper.

3. Liliana,   who is from Peru,   has got curly, blonde hair.

4. Stefan,   who is from France,   is an arachnologist.

_____

_____

_____

3 **Write a summary of the story so far.**

Four teens are studying English in England. One of the teens, Pablo, _____
_____

_____

4 **Predict what will happen in the next part of the story.**

_____

_____

_____

_____

_____

Self check 1

1 **Now I know words related to various topics . . .**

Write words or expressions related to the topics.

1. Chores _____

2. Occupations _____

3. Community service _____

4. Complaints _____

5. Movie theaters _____

2 **Now I can describe and compare people . . .**

Write words to describe people and then use them to compare your friends and you.

friendly _____

1. _I am friendlier than David but Jane is the friendliest person in the class._

2. _____

3. _____

4. _____

3 **Now I know how to . . .**

Write an example for each.

1. Give instructions: _____

2. Make polite requests: _____

3. Ask for permission: _____

4. Give biographical information: _____

4 **Now I can talk about the future . . .**

Write sentences using the cues.

1 more computers / computer programmer

In the future, there will be more computers, so I am going to be a
computer programmer.

2 few cars / car mechanic

_____

_____

3 more leisure time / talk show host

_____

_____

4 more people travel / travel agent

_____

_____

Unit 9

What should I do?

1 Write the words in the correct column.

comfortable	relaxed
happy	resentful
depressed	tired
crowded	worried
friendly	rewarding

Positive	Negative
_____	_____
_____	_____
_____	_____
_____	_____
_____	_____

2 Use the words in the box to complete the sentences. Then number the sentences to make a paragraph.

tired
happy
depressed
relaxed
resentful

_____ No one else was tired. They were all _____.

_____ I was baby-sitting until 2:00 a.m. This morning, I was really _____.

_____ They were all _____ because they did well on the test.

_____ But me, I failed. Then I was _____.

_____ Then this morning, we had a test. I was very _____ the teacher didn't tell us.

> **Could or should?**
> Use **should** to give advice. Use **could** to express a possibility or option. People often use **could** when they are not sure how someone will take the suggestion or when they're not sure it's the best suggestion.

3 Match the problem with the advice.

Problem

1. I want to work as a soccer player.
2. I have a math test tomorrow.
3. I don't want to take the bus.
4. I'm really tired.
5. Bill doesn't have e-mail.
6. I'm not hungry.

Advice

a. You could phone him.
b. You should practice a lot.
c. You should study tonight.
d. You could go to bed at 8:00.
e. You shouldn't eat now.
f. You could borrow a bicycle.

4 Circle the correct word in each conversation.

1. A: I don't want to study at the library.

   B: You (shouldn't / could) study at my house.

2. A: I need money. What (could / should) I do?

   B: You could get a part-time job.

3. A: This shirt is really ugly.

   B: Then you (could / shouldn't) wear it to school.

4. A: I don't like writing letters.

   B: You (should / shouldn't) use the telephone.

5. A: I want to get a birthday present for my friends.

   B: You (shouldn't /could) buy them a CD.

5 Unscramble the advice. Then write the advice after the correct problem.

Advice

1. breakfast / big / have / should / you / a
2. shouldn't / it / buy / you
3. sorry / say / should / you're / you
4. could / leave / you
5. should / you / him / gift / give / a
6. wear / shouldn't / you / them

Problem

a. My sister and I argued last night. _____

b. I'm really hungry. _____

c. It's my brother's birthday today. _____

d. These shoes aren't comfortable. _____

e. That shirt is too expensive. _____

f. I can't stand this movie. _____

6 Look at the three pictures. What problem is each person having? Write your advice about what they *could* or *should* do.

_____   _____   _____

LESSON B Try talking to your parents.

7 **Write the sentences. Use the verbs in parentheses.**

1. A: I've got this problem. My brother is giving me a bad time.

   B: Why don't you (try, talk) to him?

   <u>Why don't you try talking to him?</u>

2. A: I (try, talk) to him yesterday but he (ignore) me.

   _____

3. B: Well then, I (suggest, speak) with your mom.

   _____

4. A: I already did and she (suggest, be) more patient.

   _____

5. B: So what are you going to do?

   A: I (try, ignore) him and we'll see what happens.

   _____

8 **Here are three letters asking for advice about shopping. Which problem do you think is the most important? Number the problems 1 to 3 (1 = most important, 3 = least important). Give reasons for your decision.**

_____ a. Dear Donna, I don't like buying clothes at a store called Dress to Impress. The clothes are very expensive and they aren't very comfortable. But Dress to Impress is really close to my school. All my friends shop there and like the styles. What should I do?

   _____

   _____

_____ b. Dear Donna, My mother always wants to go shopping with me. She says that she pays for my clothes and she wants to help me choose them. I don't want to argue with her, but it's important to me to shop with my friends. Should I tell her she can't go shopping with me?

   _____

   _____

_____ c. Dear Donna, I hate to shop! The stores are always crowded and the salespeople usually aren't very friendly. Also, it takes me a long time to choose clothes. I want to have cool clothes but I don't want to shop. What do you think I should do?

   _____

   _____

9 **Choose one of the letters from activity 8. Write a letter giving advice to the person. Use should, shouldn't, and could in your advice.**

_____

_____

_____

_____

Go for it!
What size are you?

Answer the questions.

1. When you go to a store to buy clothes, do you know what size to ask for?
2. Do all the clothes you look at come from the same country?
3. Which countries have their own size systems?
4. How many centimeters are there in one inch?
5. Are the sizes different in each country or just the names of the sizes?
6. Women wear blouses. What do men wear?

Look at the chart. Circle the things you buy and the size you buy them in.

	United States	United Kingdom
women's blouses	8	10 (small)
	10	12 (medium)
	12	14 (large)
men's shirts	small	small
	medium	large
	large	extra large
jeans—waist size	28 inch	71 cm
	30 inch	76 cm
	32 inch	81 cm
	34 inch	86 cm
men's shoes	8	6
	9	7
	10	8
women's shoes	7	5
	8	6
	9	7
	10	8

Look at the chart and complete these statements.

1. A woman's U.K. size 10 blouse is the same as a U.S. size _____.
2. A man's U.S. size 10 shoe is the same as a U.K. size _____.
3. A woman's U.S. size 8 shoe is the same as a U.K. size _____.
4. If you have a waist size of 85 cm, you would buy U.S. jeans in size _____.
5. A man's medium shirt in the U.S. is the same as a man's _____ shirt in the U.K.
6. If you have a 28-inch waist, you would buy jeans with a _____ -centimeter waist in the U.K.

That's a big size 36!
Clothing designers keep some customers happy by making sizes bigger than they really are. A 36-inch waist on jeans used to be 36 inches, but designers often make it 38 inches so customers who have put on a bit of weight feel better about themselves!

Unit 10 LESSON A
What were you doing when the earthquake hit?

1 Match the words with the definitions.

Word	Definition
1. earthquake	a. a lot of water covering houses
2. bushfire	b. burns houses and destroys forests
3. flood	c. falling wet soil and earth
4. volcanic eruption	d. fire and hot rock coming from a mountain
5. hurricane	e. the area around a city where people live
6. mudslide	f. the center of a city
7. suburbs	g. the earth moves violently
8. coast	h. very strong wind
9. downtown	i. where the land meets the sea

2 Number the sentences to make a conversation.

_____ No, I wasn't scared, but I was dazed.

_____ The earthquake.

_____ There was an earthquake?

_____ This morning? I was sleeping. Why?

_____ Were you scared?

__1__ Michael, what were you doing at eight o'clock this morning?

_____ When what happened?

_____ Why?! You mean you were sleeping when it happened?

_____ Yes, there was. I was in the bathroom brushing my teeth.

3 Use the cues in parentheses to write the sentences or questions.

1. What (you do) when the earthquake (hit)?

   What were you doing when the earthquake hit?

2. I (watch) TV when the hurricane (arrive).

   _____

3. When the mudslide (hit), the villagers (sleep) in their huts.

   _____

4. The tourists (climb) the volcano when it (erupt).

   _____

5. The engineer (drive) across the bridge when the flood (destroy) it.

   _____

6. Where (you be) when the bushfire (start)?

   _____

4 **Use the information below to write three short paragraphs.**

Event	Doing what	Where	With whom	Felt how
1. earthquake	eating breakfast	at home	my family	not scared, surprised
2. volcano	sleeping	in a hotel	my parents	really scared
3. flood	swim	in the river	my friends	not worried, calm
4. accident	wait	at the bus stop	alone	horrified

When the earthquake hit, I was eating breakfast at home with my family. I wasn't scared at first, I was just surprised

1. _____
   _____

2. _____
   _____

3. _____
   _____

5 **Write the questions.**

1. Q: Where were you when the hurricane hit?
   A: I was at school when the hurricane hit.

2. Q: _____
   A: We were watching a movie.

3. Q: _____
   A: Everyone felt scared.

4. Q: _____
   A: When the bushfires started, we got in the car.

5. Q: _____
   A: No, there weren't any floods in Japan. There were floods in Mexico.

6 **Unscramble the sentences. The number them to make a conversation.**

_____ mom / my / and / I / home / at / were / watching / TV

_____.

_____ hit / family / what / your / doing / was / the / when / hurricane

_____?

_____ your / was / where / dad

_____?

_____ easily / could / get / he / home

_____?

_____ couldn't / he / no / night / stayed / he / the / at / last / office

_____.

_____ was / my / dad / working / still

_____.

LESSON B We met waiting for the bus.

7 Read the story. Then write the question or the answer.

Something really funny happened to me when I was on holiday last year. I was in the supermarket with my brother Dave when I saw a really beautiful woman that I thought I recognized.

Fay Swift

"Dave, isn't that Fay from the soap opera *Red Rose*?"

"You're right. Let's ask her for her autograph. Come on."

She was looking at the make-up display when we approached her.

"Excuse me, is your name Fay?" I asked.

She seemed surprised but she was very friendly.

"Yes, that's me. Nice to meet you."

"Fay, could we ask you a favor? Could we have your autograph?"

"Sure, kids. Here you are."

We were so excited. I put my autograph book in my pocket, thanked her, and we ran home to tell everyone.

Dad was taking a nap when we got home, but we woke him up to tell him. At first he didn't believe us.

"It's true. Look, here's our autograph book."

"Have you looked at this? The Fay who stars in *Red Rose* is called Fay Slift. And anyway her real name is Annabelle Refia. You got the autograph of someone else!"

Boy, did we feel dumb!

1. Q: Where were the boys when they saw Fay?

   A: _____

2. Q: _____

   A: She was looking at the make-up display.

3. Q: How did Fay react when the boys approached her?

   A: _____

4. Q: _____

   A: He was taking a nap.

5. Q: What adjectives could you use to describe how the boys felt? Write as many as possible.

   A: _____

8 Write about something interesting that happened to you or someone you know. Use *when* to talk about things that happened at the same time.

_____

_____

_____

_____

History of UFOs

Read about UFOs and circle the things people have seen in the sky.

For thousands of years, people have seen things they didn't understand in the sky. The United States Air Force first used the words *Unidentified Flying Object* to describe them. Today, everyone uses the term UFO. When people see a UFO, it is usually no more than a weather balloon or an airplane. But the Center for UFO Studies continues to receive hundreds of reports each year.

In 1947, a businessman and pilot, Kenneth Arnold, was flying near Mount Rainier, Washington, when he saw nine shiny round objects flying through the air. He told a newspaper reporter they looked like "pie plates skipping over water." The reporter used the words *flying saucer* in his story, and that's how it became the popular name for UFOs.

The Center for UFO Studies lists three kinds of contacts (or encounters) with UFOs. *Encounters of the first kind* are reports of unknown objects or lights in the sky. People have *encounters of the second kind* when a UFO leaves burn marks or other signs on the ground. People report *close encounters of the third kind* when they see or meet aliens in or near a UFO.

Read the sentences and check ✔ *True* or *False*.

	True	False

1. The United States Air Force first used the words *flying saucer*.
2. The Center for UFO Studies receives very few reports each year.
3. The term *flying saucer* was first used in 1947.
4. Kenneth Arnold is head of the Center for UFO Studies.
5. Encounters of the first kind include unknown lights or objects.
6. Encounters of the third kind include seeing or meeting aliens.

Imagine that you have seen aliens from a UFO. Describe what happened and what you did.

When I was sleeping, a UFO landed in my front yard. I got up and when I went outside.

Unit 11 LESSON A
I thought she didn't like reality shows.

1 Check ✓ the words that definitely go together. Write an ✗ for the ones that definitely don't go together. Write a ? for the ones that are possible but unusual.

	informative	exciting	educational	addictive	boring
documentary	✓	?	✓	✗	?
sitcom					
sports program					
quiz program					
cooking show					

2 Circle the correct word.

1. Melanie said to Bill: I watch sitcoms every Saturday.

   Bill says to Alex: Melanie said she (watch / watched) sitcoms every Saturday.

2. Melanie said to Bill: I don't want to watch a police drama.

   Bill says to Alex: Melanie said she didn't (wanted / want) to watch a police drama.

3. Melanie said to Bill: I love reality shows.

   Bill says to Alex: Melanie said she (loved / is loving) reality shows.

4. Melanie said to Bill: I find them addictive.

   Bill says to Alex: She said she (find / found) them addictive.

5. Melanie said to Bill: I won't be able to watch *SpyCam* tomorrow.

   Bill says to Alex: Melanie said she (wouldn't / couldn't) be able to watch *SpyCam* tomorrow.

3 Read the cartoons. Then fill in the missing words.

1. He said (that) _there was a new quiz show_ that afternoon.

2. She said (that) _____, but her TV wasn't working.

3. He said (that) _____ at his house.

4. She said (that) _____ on Tuesday afternoons.

5. He said (that) _____ for her.

6. She said (that) maybe they _____ together the following day.

4 Write the following in reported speech.

1. Maria: "When does the soccer game begin?"
   Maria asked when the soccer game began.

2. Peter: "It starts right after the news."
   _____

3. Maria: "Who will win?"
   _____

4. Peter: "I think The Tigers will win."
   _____

5. Maria: "No, I think it will be a 0-0 draw."
   _____

5 Rewrite the following to say what each person actually said.

1. He asked if I liked soap operas.
   "Do you like soap operas?"

2. I told him I did.
   _____

3. Then he asked me what my favorite was.
   _____

4. I told him that my favorite was Yellow Dragon.
   _____

5. He asked me if he could watch it with me.
   _____

6. I said that he couldn't tonight because I had chores to finish.
   _____

LESSON B **Tim said he liked documentaries.**

6 Cross out the words that do not belong.

1. music   reading   sport   work
2. favorite   sad   popular   well-liked
3. spend   visit   leisure   swim
4. collecting   socializing   dancing   Internet
5. talking   sports   hobbies   interests

7 Read the interview and answer the questions.

Interviewer:	Excuse me, we are conducting a survey about how teens spend their leisure time. Can I ask you a few questions?
Somchit:	Sure. No problem.
Interviewer:	Do you have enough leisure time?
Somchit:	No, definitely not. My life is school, homework, and chores.
Interviewer:	How do you spend your free time?
Somchit:	I love watching TV, I go dancing, I chat on the Internet, and that's about all I have time for.
Interviewer:	Of these, which is your favorite leisure activity?
Somchit.	My favorite leisure activity is dancing.
Interviewer:	And do you have time to visit friends?
Somchit:	Oh yes. Most weekends I have time to see them.
Interviewer:	Okay, fine. Thank you very much for your time. You seem to be a very busy young lady.

1. What was the first question the interviewer asked?

   He asked ___if he could ask Somchit a few questions___.

2. What was the second question?

   He asked _____

3. What was Somchit's answer?

   She said that _____

4. What was Somchit's favorite leisure activity?

   She said that _____

5. Did the interviewer ask if she had time to visit her relatives?

   No, he asked _____

6. Do you agree with the interviewer that Somchit is a busy young lady?

   _____

Go for it!
Reading a bar graph

Answer the questions.

1. Do you like advertising?

_____

2. Where do you see the most advertisements?

_____

3. Do advertisements make you want to buy certain items? Why?

_____

4. What kinds of companies spend the most on advertising?

_____

5. What is your favorite advertisement?

_____

Look at the bar graph and answer the questions.

Money Spent on Advertising

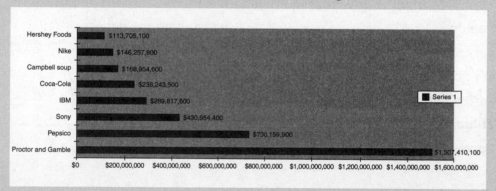

1. Which company spent about seven hundred million on advertising? _____
2. Which company spent more money, Pepsico or Coca-Cola? _____
3. Which company spent less than a hundred twenty million dollars? _____
4. Which company spent about four hundred thirty million dollars? _____
5. About how much did Campbell Soup spend? _____
6. About how much did IBM spend? _____

How much do you spend each week on different things such as entertainment, food, clothes, and transportation? Use the grid below to create a bar graph to show your spending.

Unit 12 LESSON A
If you go to the party, you'll have a great time.

1 Complete the sentences. Use the words in the box.

tattoo	regret	charge	decently	permission

1. Did you get _____ to bring a guest?

2. I got a _____ on my leg and my mom got mad. Real mad!

3. My dad is always saying that if I don't work hard at school, I'll _____ it.

4. You have to dress _____ to get into the disco. No jeans, no T-shirts.

5. Unless you bring your student card, they'll _____ you extra.

2 Match the phrases to make sentences.

1. What will you do
2. Unless he gets permission,
3. If she doesn't go,
4. If we don't dress decently,
5. Will they let him
6. What will happen

a. he can't go the dance.
b. bring a guest?
c. if they arrive late?
d. if you're bored tonight?
e. they'll send us home.
f. she'll be miserable.

3 Number the sentences to make a conversation.

_____ I failed my test. If I fail another test tomorrow afternoon, mom says I have to stay home.

_____ I got into trouble today.

__1__ I'm looking forward to the basketball game tomorrow night.

_____ I'm not sure I really want to go.

_____ Miserable? Why?

_____ Stay home? That's too bad. I know, let's study together tonight!

_____ Study together? You can help me with my homework?

_____ Sure. We can study. You can pass your test. We can go to the basketball game!

_____ What kind of trouble?

_____ Yes, I'm sure it will be great, but I'm miserable.

_____ You're not sure? Why not? It will be great.

4 Complete the sentences. Use the phrases in the box.

will be late	will laugh at you	will never stop talking	will take it away
won't study	for your test	will tell you to stop	

1. Don't talk in class. If you do, the teacher _____.
2. Don't bring candy to school. If you do, the teacher _____.
3. Don't watch TV tonight. If you do, you _____.
4. Don't walk too slowly. If you do, you _____.
5. Don't dye your hair blue. If you do, people _____.
6. Don't ask about his children. If you do, he _____.

5 Circle the correct word.

1. If you don't try, you will (regret / please) it.
2. Don't (remember / forget) your school pass. You need it!
3. If you don't dress (decently / jeans), we can't go.
4. What will we do if you get (danced / bored) at the dance?
5. We need special (problem / permission) to go to the dance.
6. What will (happen / happened) if you don't go to school today?

6 Complete the sentences with the correct tense of the verb in parentheses.

1. If you (go) __go_____ to the party, you (have to wear) __will have to wear__ decent clothes.
2. Unless Hector (work) _____ harder, he (fail) _____ the exam.
3. I (not go) _____, unless you (come) _____ with me.
4. You (be) _____ in trouble if you (break) _____ the rules.
5. If it (rain) _____, we (have to) _____ postpone the game.
6. If nobody (bring) _____ a friend, there (not be) _____ enough people at the party.

LESSON B If you drop out of school now, you won't go to college later.

7 Look at the four pictures. Make predictions about what will happen.

_____		_____	
_____		_____	
_____		_____	
_____		_____	

1. If you watch TV late at night, you will wake up late. _____
2. _____
3. _____
4. _____

8 Read the email. Then answer the questions.

Subject: New job

From: Ahmed

To: Gary

I was surprised to hear you're planning to get a new job. I don't think you should leave. They pay you $13 an hour. If you look in the newspaper, you'll see that's more than most places pay. Also, if you leave without permission, you will pay a charge. If you get another job, you won't get such good hours. Now you can work after school and on weekends. I'm going to see you next week. Let's talk. If we do, I'm sure you will stay at the coffee shop.

1. Why was Ahmed surprised that Gary wants a new job?

    _____

2. What was Ahmed's advice to Gary?

    _____

3. If Gary leaves without permission, what will happen?

    _____

4. When does Gary work?

    _____

5. When is Ahmed going to see Gary?

    _____

Go for it!
Reading a line graph

Read the article and study the graph. Then answer the questions.

Twenty years ago, very few American high schools played soccer, a game known as football in much of the rest of the world. Most students were interested in baseball, basketball, and American football. However, soccer is quickly becoming the most popular sport in many high schools. The line graph below shows the growth of interest in soccer among boys and girls in one American high school.

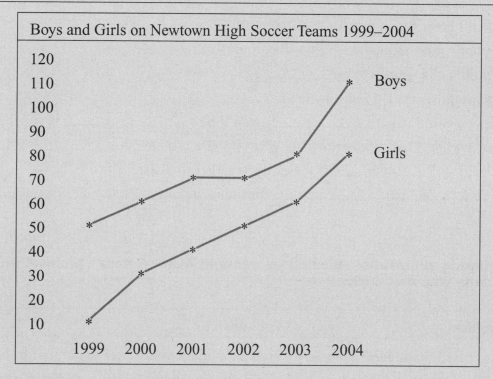

Boys and Girls on Newtown High Soccer Teams 1999–2004

1. In which year were there 50 girls on the Newtown High soccer team? _____
2. In which year were there 50 boys on the Newtown High soccer team? _____
3. How many boys were on the team in 2002? _____
4. Which team had the same number of players two years in a row? _____
5. How many boys and girls were playing soccer in 2004? _____
6. In what year was there the greatest difference between the number of boys and girls on a team? _____

Write a paragraph about a sport that you know. Use the article as a model to describe how it has become more popular in recent years. Give reasons why.

_____

_____

_____

_____

Review 3

1 Complete the conversation. Use the words in the box.

fun	soap opera	crowded
organized	coast record	different
hurricane	worry	miserable

Liza: OK, everyone. What are we going to do for the holiday weekend? Let's do something (1) _____.

Jim: We could go to the mountains, or to the (2) _____.

Deng: Everybody goes to the beach. It will be too (3) _____.

Liza: The mountains sound (4) _____.

Natalia: But If we go away, I'll miss my (5) _____.

Liza: Well, you could (6) _____ it. You'll be (7) _____ if you stay at home.

Deng: OK, but what if the weather is bad? What if there is a (8) _____ or a flood?

Jim: Don't (9) _____. I'll check the weather forecast.

Liza: OK, so let's get (10) _____ for the mountains.

2 Natalia is talking to Liza about the holiday weekend. Match Natalia's problem with Liza's advice. Then write your own advice.

Natalia's problem	Liza's advice
1. It's going to be cold and miserable.	a. You should ask your sister to help with them.
2. I have a lot of chores to do at home.	b. Do it all tonight and then you will have a free weekend.
3. My mom won't let me go, I'm sure.	c. You should take lots of sweaters and warm clothes.
4. I have too much homework.	d. You should talk to her and explain that it's not dangerous.

1. _____

2. _____

3. _____

4. _____

3 Read the weather forecast. Then rewrite it in reported speech.

Here is the weather forecast for the holiday weekend. The general outlook is good. The weather on the coast will be hot and sunny with highs of 25 degrees Celsius. In the mountains, there is a possibility of thunderstorms in the afternoons.

14° C 58° F   20° C 45° F

They said that
(1) ___the general outlook was good___ for the holiday weekend. They said the weather on the coast (2) _____ hot and sunny. In the mountains, they said that (3) _____ a possibility of thunderstorms in the afternoons.

4 Liza wrote an e-mail to Natalia when she got back from the mountains. Write the verbs in the correct tense.

Hi Natalia,

How (be) 1. _____ your weekend? We (have) 2. _____ a miserable time. You (be) 3. _____ right not to go!
First, Jim said that he (will) 4. _____ buy all the food, but he (forget) 5. _____. Can you believe it! Then, when we (put up) 6. _____ the tent, it (start) 7. _____ to rain. And it rained and rained all weekend. You should (try sleep) 8. _____ in a wet sleeping bag. Ugh! Unless we (stay) 9. _____ in a hotel, I (not go) 10. _____ to the mountains ever again.

5 Write Natalia's reply. Use the following phrases.

| great time |
| movies - action film - exciting |
| TV - reality program - interesting |
| party - new boyfriend–cute |

_____

_____

_____

_____

_____

Unit 13 LESSON A
How long have you been rehearsing?

1 How would you or someone you know feel after doing these activities? Check the possible answers.

	tired	out of breath	bored	annoyed	stressed out
running					
playing pool					
rehearsing					
playing the guitar					

2 Fill in the blanks. Use *since* or *for*.

1. I've been practicing _____ 10:30.

2. Mario has been running _____ 15 minutes.

3. Sarah has been sleeping _____ 9:00.

4. Dale has been talking on the phone _____ five minutes.

5. Louie has been studying Chinese _____ he was six years old.

6. The coach has been watching the players _____ ten minutes.

3 Write about the four pictures. How long has each person been doing something?

It is now three o'clock.

1. _____

2. _____

3. _____

4. _____

4 Write the questions.

1. Q: ___How long has he been standing there?___

   A: He has been standing there for four hours.

2. Q: _____

   A: I've been riding a bicycle since I was ten years old.

3. Q: _____

   A: She has been walking for five hours.

4. Q: _____

   A: I've been watching TV since 7:00.

5. Q: _____

   A: He has been waiting for the train for an hour.

6. Q: _____

   A: We have been playing soccer together since 2003.

5 Number the sentences to make a conversation.

_____ Thank you.

_____ Only six months! I'm surprised. You're very good.

__1__ Hey, you're good at pool.

_____ Oh, for about four years.

_____ And you? How long have you been playing?

_____ How long have you been playing?

_____ Much less than you. Only about six months.

_____ Four years! That's much longer than I.

6 Write sentences in the correct tense.

1. study Italian	1999 to 2003
2. play guitar	2003 to now
3. work at this school	1996 to now
4. live in the United States	2002 to 2003
5. go to dancing classes	2000 to now
6. wait	7.00 a.m. to now

> The past simple is used when an action is completed.
> **I studied** French for five years. (I don't study French now.)
> The present perfect continuous is used when the action is still taking place.
> **I have been studying** French for five years. (I am still studying French.)

1. ___I studied Italian for four years.___

2. _____

3. _____

4. _____

5. _____

6. _____

LESSON B **I'm the adventurous type.**

7 Unscramble the words. Then write them under the correct photograph.

yinigsdkv   korc giinlcmb   aaiykkgn   asbuc ginvid   eikgktnr   aeiglplrn

_____   _____   _____   _____   _____

8 Read the article. Underline all the verbs in the present perfect continuous and circle all the verbs in the present perfect.

Multi-talented or Just Crazy?

Twenty-year-old Danny Haslett is an extreme-sport freak. He has won competitions in rock climbing and kayaking and has been selected for the national paragliding team.

Interviewer:	So, Danny, I've been doing some research on you and I believe that you have tried 12 different extreme sports.
Danny:	Really! I didn't know that! I haven't counted them.
Interviewer:	Is there any extreme sport that you haven't tried?
Danny:	I've never tried cave diving. I've been thinking about it but I can never find the time.
Interviewer:	Which is your favorite extreme sport?
Danny:	I love them all but paragliding is my favorite.
Interviewer:	How long have you been paragliding?
Danny:	For about 8 years.
Interviewer:	Is it dangerous? Have you ever had an accident?
Danny:	Yes, it is dangerous but I have been doing it for 8 years and I have never had an accident. However, you have to have a good instructor and the best equipment.
Interviewer:	Finally, Danny, do you have any advice for our readers?
Danny:	Sure. If you want to do something, just go for it! But find a good teacher first.

9 Write an article about someone you know who has an interesting job or hobby. Say what the person does and how long he or she has been doing it.

_____

_____

_____

_____

North American time zones

Scientists, pilots, and weather forecasters in the United States use a 24-hour clock instead of the 12-hour clock that most other people use. This clock uses Greenwich Mean Time (GMT) as a starting point. Greenwich Mean Time is the time in Greenwich, England.

To change GMT to local time, we must know the difference between GMT and local time. As you go east from Greenwich, you add hours to the current GMT. As you go west, you subtract hours. In the United States, during the summer, some areas use Daylight Savings Time. In these states, people set their clocks forward one hour so that they can enjoy a longer evening before it gets dark. The abbreviations EDT, CDT and MDT indicate Daylight Savings Time in three parts of the U.S.

Here is a chart showing the time zones across North America.

	Standard Time	difference	Daylight Savings Time	difference
Atlantic		−4 hours		
Eastern	EST	−5 hours	EDT	−4 hours
Central	CST	−6 hours	CDT	−5 hours
Mountain	MST	−7 hours	MDT	−6 hours
Alaska		−9 hours		
Hawaii		−10 hours		

Read the article again and answer the questions.

1. What people in the United States use a 24-hour clock?
   _____

2. What does EST mean?
   _____

3. What do you think MST means?
   _____

4. Do Alaska and Hawaii use Daylight Savings Time?
   _____

5. New York City is in the Eastern Time Zone. If it's 9:00 p.m. in Greenwich, England, on December 1, what time is it in New York City?
   _____

6. New York City uses Daylight Savings Time in the summer. If it is seven o'clock in the evening in Greenwich, England, on July 1, what time is it in New York City?
   _____

Unit 14 LESSON A
Could you turn it down a little?

1 Match the phrases.

1. Would you mind cleaning   a. the music?
2. Would you mind getting out   b. of the bathroom?
3. Would you mind turning down   c. the lid on the trashcan?
4. Would you mind putting   d. feet?
5. Would you mind getting   e. up?
6. Would you mind moving your   f. the yard?

2 Rewrite these sentences more politely using *Would you mind* . . .

Impolite / informal   **Polite / formal**

1. Sit down.   Would you mind sitting down?
2. Help me.   _____
3. Go to the store for me.   _____
4. Clean the car.   _____
5. Turn down the music.   _____
6. Don't talk.   _____

3 Circle the correct words in each sentence.

1. We're (supposed to / not supposed to) make noise. The baby is sleeping.
2. We're (supposed to / not supposed to) wait ten minutes. He's finishing his homework.
3. We're (supposed to / not supposed to) phone her. She's practicing for the concert.
4. We're (supposed to / not supposed to) keep pets. She hates cats and dogs.
5. We're (supposed to / not supposed to) clear the fire exit so that people can escape.
6. We're (supposed to / not supposed to) play music loudly. It's too late.

> **Is would you mind a question?**
> When someone asks **Would you mind . .**
> . .,its usually a polite way to give an
> order. Its not really a question that
> you are expected to react to negatively
> unless you have a good reason.

4 Read the first conversation. Then write similar conversations using the phrases in the box.

| Would you mind . . . -ing . . . | Would you . . . | Could you . . . | Do you think you could . . . |

1. Complaint: It's 11:00 p.m. and the music is too loud.
   Request: <u>Could you turn off the music, please?</u>
   Reason: <u>You're not supposed to play music after 10:00.</u>
   Response: <u>Sorry, I'll turn it off.</u>

2. Complaint: Your neighbor has parked his car across the driveway.
   Request: _____
   Reason: _____
   Response: _____

3. Complaint: There is garbage in the hallway.
   Request: _____
   Reason: _____
   Response: _____

4. Complaint: Your neighbor has left the faucet dripping.
   Request: _____
   Reason: _____
   Response: _____

5 Check ✓ the sentences that are correct. Put an ✗ next to the sentences that are not correct and rewrite them.

1. <u>✗</u> Are you supposed to keep pets?
   <u>Are you allowed to keep pets?</u>

2. _____ Would you mind putting the lid in the trashcan?
   _____

3. _____ Do you think you could turn the music down?
   _____

4. _____ Could you clear the fire exit?
   _____

5. _____ There's a rule about none pets in the building.
   _____

6. _____ Would you mind eating the trash?
   _____

LESSON B **Sorry about that.**

6 Read the letter. Then write the question or the answer.

Tuesday, 23rd June
Dear Sir:

Last Friday, I bought a new memory stick for my computer at your shop. When I got
home I discovered that it was not working, so I went back to the shop yesterday and
spoke to your sales assistant, Trudy Green. Unfortunately, Miss Green was not very
helpful. She said that she could not give me a new memory stick because I did not
have the receipt. I pointed out that the name of your shop was written on the
package but she still refused to give me a new one. I then asked if it was possible
to see the manager, but she told me you were busy and I would have to make an
appointment.

I have to say that I do not think that this is very good service. First, you sell
me a product that does not work, second, your sales assistant was not at all
helpful, and finally, I was not allowed to speak to you.

Would you mind contacting me immediately by telephone (356 234 143) and delivering
to my house a new memory stick.

Yours sincerely,

Emma Bartlet

1. Q: _____

   A: Emma bought a memory stick for her computer.

2. Q: When did Emma try to return the memory stick?

   A: _____

3. Q: Why wouldn't the sales assistant give Emma a new memory stick?

   A: _____

4. Q: Why didn't Emma speak to the manager in the shop?

   A: _____

5. Q: Who do you think was correct, the sales assistant or Emma? Give your reasons.

   A: _____

7 Write a similar letter complaining about something that you've bought that doesn't work.

_____

_____

_____

_____

Go for it!
From apartments to houses

Read the article. What terms and places are used for *homes*?

_____

_____

Read the article again and circle *True* or *False*. Then rewrite the false statements.

Many people dream of moving out of an apartment and into their own house. When World War II ended in 1945, thousands of returning soldiers were ready to get married and start families, and they needed places to live. There weren't enough homes for them. Some of them crowded into their families' apartments. Others lived in attics, garages, or basements. But these soldiers had fought a war for their country, and they wanted something better.

In 1947, Abraham Levitt and Sons started to build small homes on an old potato farm on Long Island, near New York City. In four years, they built 17,447 houses. They named this new place Levittown. The government helped the soldiers borrow money to purchase houses there. For many families, it was cheaper to buy a house (only $58 a month) than to live in an apartment in the

city. The families who moved in there were living the "American Dream."

One early buyer said, "I bought a new 1950 Levitt Ranch Home. Each house had GE appliances, a Bendix washer, and its own big 12-inch Admiral television set. Wow, this was a real selling feature, especially for me and my wife. To be able to move into a new home with all these new luxury items was unbelievable."

1. World War II ended in 1950.	True	False
2. Levitt built expensive houses.	True	False
3. The Levitt company built over 15,000 houses in four years.	True	False
4. Levitt houses were cheaper than New York apartments.	True	False
5. Buyers in Levittown had to purchase their own appliances.	True	False

If you were going to buy a new home, what would you like included? Write a description of your dream home. Use expressions like the following.

It would have . . . _____

There would be . . . _____

It wouldn't be . . . _____

Unit 15 LESSON A
Why don't you get her a scarf?

1 Read the sentences and correct the spelling mistakes.

1. A dictonary is too boring as a gift. __dictionary__

2. Have you ever given your sister earings? _____

3. Last Christmas she got a bycicle and a photo album. _____

4. Why don't you buy him some sunglases? _____

5. Have you ever gotten an incence burner as a gift? _____

6. A kiten would be a fun gift. _____

2 Use the words to write questions.

1. you / see / Britney Spears __Have you ever seen Britney Spears?__

2. your father / give you / expensive present? _____

3. we / give grandmother / photo album? _____

4. the twins / get / different clothes? _____

5. you / get / kitten / as a gift? _____

6. I / give you / a live concert DVD? _____

3 Use the clues to complete the crossword puzzle.

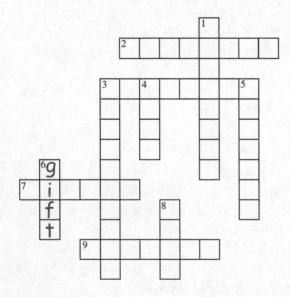

Down

1. an expensive kind of pen

3. People who plan to get married have an _____ party.

4. Take off your shoes and put them on the shoe _____.

5. She doesn't have a car. She rides a motor _____.

6. something that you give someone on their birthday

8. I gave my parents some _____ glasses.

Across

2. something for one person's use only

3. jewelry for your ears

7. a baby cat

9. I can smell the _____ burner.

4 Match the gifts to the people and write a short conversation about each one.

birthday

engagement

anniversary

graduation

1. A: _Why don't you get him a digital camera?_
   B: _That's too expensive. I'll get him a soccer ball._
2. A: _____
   B: _____
3. A: _____
   B: _____
4. A: _____
   B: _____

5 Write the questions.

1. Q: _Have you ever gotten a digital camera?_
   A: Yes, I got a digital camera for my birthday.
2. Q: _____
   A: No, a watch is too personal.
3. Q: _____
   A: No, a DVD is too ordinary.
4. Q: _____
   A: Yes, I gave my parents a photo album for their wedding anniversary.
5. Q: _____
   A: No, a bicycle is too ordinary for his graduation.

6 Circle the correct word.

1. When is your parents' (birthday / anniversary)?

2. Have you ever gotten a (earrings / kitten) as a gift?

3. No, that's not (special / gift) enough.

4. My (parents' / friends') engagement party is next month.

5. Her (grandparent's / grandparents') wedding anniversary was last week.

6. I gave him a motor scooter (last / next) birthday.

It's the best gift I've ever received.

7 **Number the sentences to make a conversation.**

____ A goldfish is a good pet. But doesn't Julie have a cat?

____ A pet? I'm not sure. Some people don't like pets.

____ But she loves them. Maybe I could get her a dog.

__1__ Hi, Alan. What are you going to get Julie for her birthday?

____ I don't know. I could get her a pet.

____ If a snake is too scary, how about a goldfish?

____ Maybe you're right. How about a snake?

____ Oh no! A snake is too scary!

____ Well, a dog is too difficult to take care of.

____ Well, don't you think the cat might eat the goldfish?

____ Yes, she does.

8 **Laura is thinking about her father's birthday and writes an e-mail to her sister. What's the problem with each idea? Write a reply giving your advice.**

```
Subject: Dad's birthday
Date: June 18th
From: Laura
To: Lisa

Dear Lisa, I can't decide what to get Dad for his birthday. He loves watching TV,
but I don't have enough money to buy a new big one. I could get him a shirt or
some other clothes, but that's not a very interesting gift. He sometimes plays
tennis on the weekends. I could get him some tennis balls, but I'd like to get
him a more personal gift. A tie? No, that doesn't cost enough. I know! I'll get
him something for his home office. Maybe he'd like a new chair. What do you
think, Lisa?

Laura
```

1. a television _____

2. clothes _____

3. tennis balls _____

4. a tie _____

_____

_____

_____

9 **Think of a good gift for a friend. Write a note saying what you think about the gift and why it would be good for him or her.**

_____

_____

_____

Go for it!
A personal budget

Calculate Laura's income, multiplying the weeks where necessary. Then add up the totals.

Laura's income for April		
source	amount	total for month
allowance from parents	$5.00 a week	$20.00
birthday money	$25.00	
baby-sitting	$10.00 a week	
part-time job	$15.00 a week	
Total income		

Laura's expenses for April		
source	amount	total for month
movie every Friday night	$5.00 a week	$20.00
new clothes	$50.00	
birthday present for Alice	$20.00	
pizza party with friends	$35.00	
new CD	$15.00	
Total expenses		

Answer the questions.

1. Which was bigger, Laura's income or her expenses?

   _____

2. How much money did Laura have at the end of the month?

   _____

3. Where did most of Laura's money come from in April?

   _____

4. What was Laura's largest expense in April?

   _____

5. If Laura wants to make $60 more a month, how many extra afternoons will she need to work? _____

6. How much money can she save if she goes to movies only twice a month?

   _____

Unit 16 LESSON A
Have you ever been to an amusement park?

1 Match the words. Then use the words in sentences.

1. dinosaur   a. cage
2. amusement   b. museum
3. shark   c. skeleton
4. science   d. simulator
5. space shuttle   e. park

1. _____
2. _____
3. _____
4. _____
5. _____

2 Number the sentences to make a conversation.

_____ Different? Like what?

___1___ Hi, Marcie. Do you feel like doing something different today?

_____ I haven't seen the new amusement park.

_____ I saw the sharks last week.

_____ Oh no. It's not too expensive. Let's go!

_____ Oh yes. I went to the space museum last week.

_____ Really? How about we go to the aquarium and see the new sharks?

_____ That's two things. What haven't you seen?

_____ The new amusement park? It's fantastic, but it's expensive.

_____ Well, have you seen the new space museum?

3 Combine the sentences using *that*.

1. I went to the new aquarium. It was opened last year.
   I went to the new aquarium that was opened last year.

2. Have you ever seen the reptile park? It's next to the zoo.
   _____

3. Last year, we visited an amusement park. It had free rides all day.
   _____

4. I don't want to go to that zoo. It has really small cages for the animals.
   _____

5. John wants to go to a museum. The museum has a space shuttle simulator.
   _____

4 Write questions and answers about the four pictures. Use adjectives from the box.

frightening	scary	exciting	boring	interesting

1. Q: _Have you ever been on a rollercoaster?_
   A: _No, it's too frightening._
2. Q: _____
   A: _____
3. Q: _____
   A: _____
4. Q: _____
   A: _____

5 Fill in the blanks using *have, haven't, ever, never,* or *been.*

1. Q: Have you __ever__ been to the zoo?
   A: Yes, I __have.__
2. Q: Have you ever _____ to the science museum?
   A: No, I _____.
3. Q: _____ you ever been to see the space shuttle simulator?
   A: No, I've _____ been there.
4. Q: Have you _____ been to the doctor?
   A: Yes, I _____.
5. Q: Grandma, _____ you ever been to a water park?
   A: No, I _____. What's a water park?

6 Match the questions and answers.

1. Have you ever been to the history museum?
2. Has she ever been to the new zoo?
3. Has he ever been to your school?
4. Have John and Alex ever been to the space shuttle simulator?
5. Has Alice ever been to the aquarium?
6. Have you ever been to my house?

a. Yes, she has. And she saw the elephants!
b. Yes, she has. And she saw the new shark tank.
c. No, but I've been to the science museum.
d. No, they have never been there.
e. No, I haven't. But I'm coming to your party tonight!
f. Yes, he has. And he enjoyed it a lot.

LESSON B It's been a great weekend.

7 Choose four places that you have never visited. Why would you like to visit them?

1. _I have never been to an aquarium. I would like to see a real octopus._
2. _____
3. _____
4. _____
5. _____

8 Read about Taiwan. Then answer the *True* or *False* statements. Write the correct answers for the false statements.

Have you ever visited Taiwan? If not, you should start your trip in Taiwan's biggest city, Taipei. It is an outstanding city, full of interesting things to do. The official language is Mandarin Chinese, but English-speaking guides are easy to find. You can go to museums, go shopping, visit an amusement park, or just sit and watch people.

Taipei

A good place to buy souvenirs is the Chinese Handicraft Mart. Small stores in the Hsimenting section also sell clothes and shoes. Other small shops around Dinghao sell books and sports items. In Taiwan, these small stores are usually much less expensive than the big stores. Most stores are open until 9:30 or later.

One afternoon, you should visit Yangmingshan National Park, just north of Taipei. It is a beautiful, uncrowded place to walk and has pretty lakes, trees, and flowers. There are also many different kinds of birds, as well as wild monkeys. Taiwan offers the visitor many fantastic places to go and beautiful things to see.

1. Taipei is Taiwan's biggest city.   True   False
   _____

2. The official language of Taiwan is English.   True   False
   _____

3. There is an amusement park in Taiwan.   True   False
   _____

4. Stores in Taiwan close around 8:00.   True   False
   _____

5. Yangmingshan National Park is south of Taipei.   True   False
   _____

Go for it!
World travel

Read the letters from two travelers. Then answer the questions.

How do you like to travel?

This month, our topic is "How do you like to travel?" The following are letters from two travelers with quite different opinions.

There is only one reason to travel, and that is to see and understand the world's history and culture. Before I travel, I do a lot of research to find out what is worth seeing and doing in each place. I start with the museums and art galleries. For some museums and galleries, I book tickets on the Internet so I won't miss anything or waste time waiting. Then I try to find out about old important buildings. I also read old stories and novels about places I visit. It's very romantic. I don't like any surprises when I travel. Mark

The only reason to travel is to meet people and do unexpected things. When I go to a new place, I like to stay at cheap hotels where I can meet other travelers with backpacks. These people are better than any guidebook because they can tell you what is worth seeing and doing, for example, where the newest restaurants and clubs are. I don't like looking at old museums and art galleries. It's better to see these things in books. I'd rather go to the beach or on a mountain hike any day! Liz

1. Would it be a good idea for Liz and Mark to travel together?

   _____

2. What does Mark like to do when he travels?

   _____

3. What does Liz like to do when she travels?

   _____

4. Why doesn't Liz like museums?

   _____

5. How does Mark avoid wasting time?

   _____

6. Who do you think spends more money when they travel, Liz or Mark?

   _____

Write your own letter about what you like to do when you travel.

_____

_____

_____

_____

Review 4

1 Read the conversation about *Jim's Gift*. Then fill in the missing words for *Liza's Gift* and write about *Deng's Gift*. Use the words in the boxes.

It is the end of the school year and Jim, Liza, and Deng are moving to different schools. They are planning a trip and are going to buy gifts for each other.

Jim's Gift

Deng: Why don't we buy Jim a ticket for the The Streets concert?

Liza: What! That's way too expensive.

Deng: OK. Let me see. He has been taking guitar lessons for two years. What about a guitar magazine?

Liza: Great idea.

Liza's Gift

lessons	name	been	perfect	expensive

Deng: Well, Liza has (1) _____ taking computer (2) _____ for a year. What about a hand-held computer?

Jim: Come on! They are far too (3) _____.

Deng: Let me think. What about a personalized mouse mat with her (4) _____ written on it?

Jim: (5) _____.

Deng's Gift

physical education classes	running shoes	running shorts

Liza: _____

Jim: _____

Liza: _____

Jim: _____

2 Number the sentences to make a conversation.

_____ Deng: I agree. The museum's not much fun. Has anyone been to the zoo recently?

_____ Deng: No. Everyone likes animals. And I believe they have a cute baby panda.

_____ Liza: Sounds great. What do you think, Jim?

_____ Liza: Have you ever been to the museum?

_____ Jim: OK. Let's go to the zoo.

_____ Deng: Which museum?

_____ Jim: No, museums are boring. And it's too far from home.

_1_ Jim: OK. Where shall we go?

_____ Liza: You know. The museum that has the dinosaur exhibit.

_____ Jim: The zoo! That's for little kids.

3 There are many rules at the zoo. Write the *Request* or *Reason* using the phrases in the box.

pick up that paper   walking on the path   smoke   turning off your radio   use flash photography

Request

1. Would you please stop that?
2. Would you please stop using your camera?
3. Please, would you _____?
4. Would you mind _____?
5. Would you please put out that cigarette?
6. Would you mind _____?

Reason

You're not supposed to feed the animals.

_____

You're not supposed drop litter.

You're not supposed to walk on the grass.

_____

You're not supposed to make a lot of noise.

4 Liza writes in her diary every day. She doesn't use full sentences. She writes in note form. Read the diary entry and then write it in full sentences.

Saturday July 5

Morning: Bought gifts for Jim and Deng. Guitar magazine for Jim and neat running shorts for Deng. Gave me a cool mouse mat. Good friends.

Afternoon: Went to zoo. Not much fun. So many rules! Felt sorry for the animals. Like a prison. Real cute baby panda.

Evening: Went to movies. Great film—very funny. Said good-bye to Jim and Deng. Sad. Cried a little. Will miss them.

_____

_____

_____

_____

_____

_____

5 Write the questions or the answers.

1. Q: Why did the teens buy each other presents?
   A: _____

2. Q: _____
   A: They bought her some running shorts.

3. Q: _____
   A: Because he thinks museums are boring.

4. Q: How long have they been trying to breed giant pandas at the zoo?
   A: _____

5. Q: Have you ever had to say good-bye to a good friend? What did you do? How did you feel?
   A: _____

My reading journal 2

Complete the journal page.

1 Draw lines to match the columns to make statements that are true about the story.

1. Mrs. Pitt	normally live in the United States	and has eight very hairy legs!
2. Mr. Pitt	lives in a glass tank in Billy and Junko's house,	and he also plays rock music.
3. Billy Wright	cooks great pizzas	but want to buy a holiday home in Bristol.
4. Stomper	plays the violin,	but is not a very friendly woman.
5. Pablo	is married to a 'difficult' woman	but he likes Sophie more!
6. Mr. And Mrs. Sterling	likes Stomper,	and is the most wonderful girl in the world.
7. Sophie	buys and sells houses	but he likes living in his house.

2 Think about the story. What event in the story surprised you?

3 Use the organizer to show the plot of *Spider*. Write an important event that happened in the story in each box. If you need to, use your notebook to add events.

```
1
▼
2
▼
3
▼
4
```

4 Write a short book review of *Spider*. Use the notes from your reading journals to help you describe what happened. Then tell why you liked or did not like the story.

Book Review: *Spider*

_____

_____

_____

_____

_____

_____

Self check 2

1 Now I know words related to various topics . . .

Write words or expressions related to the topics.

1. Disasters

_____

2. TV shows

_____

3. Requests

_____

4. Special attractions

_____

5. Gifts

_____

2 Now I can talk about consequences . . .

Complete the statements and then write a complete sentence of your own.

1. If I get a tattoo, _____

2. If I don't do my homework, _____

3. _____ my parents will be mad.

4. _____, I'll look cool.

5. _____, _____ .

3 Now I know how to . . .

Write an example for each.

1. Make suggestions: _____

2. Complain: _____

3. Give advice: _____

4. Say how I feel. _____

5. Make polite requests: _____

4 Now I can talk about what people say . . .

1. My sister said, "The new soap opera is really coo."
   My sister said that the new soap opera was really cool.

2. Jill said, "I don't have anything to wear for the part."

_____

3. "When is the show?" Paul asked.

_____

4. "Can we watch the game at your house?" Steve asked me.

_____

5. "Will you be coming home late?" my mom asked me.

_____